I Am the Maker of all sweetened possum

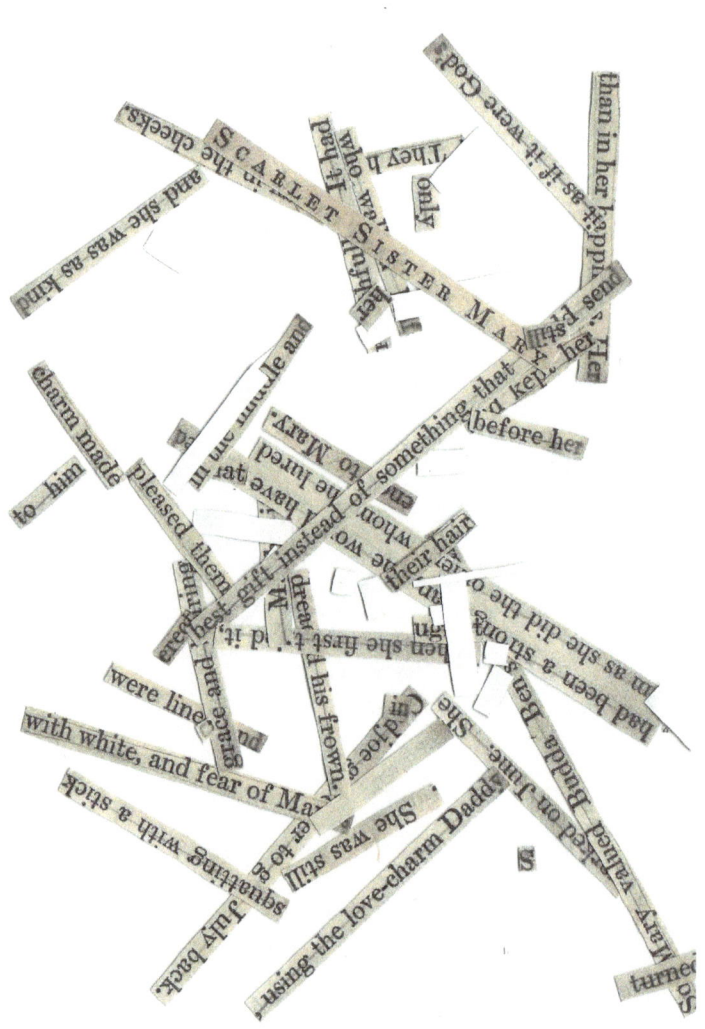

I Am the Maker
of all sweetened possum

poetry found in Scarlet Sister Mary

james w. moore

SILVER BIRCH PRESS
LOS ANGELES, CALIFORNIA

© copyright 2014, james w. moore

ISBN-13: 978-0615945095

ISBN-10: 0615945090

FIRST EDITION, March 2014

Email: silver@silverbirchpress.com

Web: silverbirchpress.com

Blog: silverbirchpress.wordpress.com

Cover Design: james w. moore

Mailing Address:
Silver Birch Press
P.O. Box 29458
Los Angeles, CA 90029

by way of introduction
james w. moore

1. the beginning
"You should. Do it. Now."
that's the body of the email by my friend and fellow poet David Krilivsky telling me about the *Found Poetry Review*'s National Poetry Month initiative: the Pulitzer Remix—poets selecting one of 85 Pulitzer Prize-winning works of fiction and creating 30 found poems from its pages.

when the *Found Poetry Review* editor emails me back, this is how it appears in my gmail:

"Found, me"

and i think maybe that's so.

2. the remainder
by the time i email, there are only five of the 85 Pulitzer Prize-winning works of fiction left. my first choices of a Faulkner or Wharton or Chabon have long since been selected. i recognize none of these remaining five, but, i rationalize, maybe not knowing the text ahead of time is actually better. plus, *what* i'll be remixing is of less importance to me than the fact *that* i'll be remixing. so i select the one that sounds the most interesting to me based on its meager Wikipedia entry: a book about a community of black people living on a plantation at the start of the 20th century, written by a white woman who lived on a plantation just after the start of the 20th century: a book that, when it was awarded the Pulitzer, motivated one judge to walk off in protest. yeah, that was the book for me:

Scarlet Sister Mary by Julia Peterkin.

3. to read or not to read
i decide not to read *Scarlet Sister Mary* before remixing it. i don't want my poems to be influenced by the story or Julia Peterkin's writing. the best weapon against that, i reason, is ignorance.

4. let's get this out of the way
i feel that all words should start with the same weight, at least in appearance. moist and luminescence may have different weights in meaning, but if they have the same base appearance, it gives me more freedom to make a word stand out just by adding a Capital letter.

5. to read or not to read (part two)
i decide to read *Scarlet Sister Mary*. i don't want my work to simply become an edited version of the novel. the best weapon against that, i reason, is knowing what came before. i made the right choice—not only am i now aware of what's on the pages, but i'm properly humbled by Peterkin's language, which alternates between blunt and florid within two sentences.

Scarlet Sister Mary is a heavy book; its themes are huge and universal: good, evil, God, Satan, heaven, hell, gender, race. comparatively, the themes in my [non-found] poetry are more local, based on observation, things i've actually seen or felt, footsteps in which i've actually walked: more like the universe based on what i've seen of it.

to make something that illustrates my locality using Peterkin's universality is what i fear most. i want the poems to sound like things i'd write, even if i'm writing in someone else's words. i feel daunted and i don't know where to begin. feeling like the project is too wide open, i ask my friends and family to restrict my options by assigning me page numbers with which to work.

6. intertextual criticism or how i learned to stop worrying and write the poem
i don't want to be a critic of Peterkin and *Scarlet Sister Mary*. the first page of her novel is a real doozy to this 21st century reader, as it describes the "best kind of black people." my first 'remix' of the page might as well be called "i think Peterkin's writing is racist." it was poetry as criticism, and perhaps even unfair, revisionist history criticism. the truth is more complicated. i change the first words of my first remix from "The black people are the best black people" to "The people believe they are the best people," and the poem "the fine mechanics" is born.

7. elementary and out of control

found poetry is a mystery to me. there is nothing Lost in the first place; all the words are there on the page for a work that already exists. to find something else, something wholly new that merely uses some of the words on that page, can feel impossible.

i had never written found poetry prior to this month. looking back, some of my work has the markings of found poetry (sampled lines from class lectures, magazines, and nutrition labels), but this will be the first time i create found poetry as such. David had given me some examples, and i was immediately drawn to the puzzle-like nature of the work, as well as to the sense that something has been redacted and left behind. it was David who suggested i begin by just looking at the page, trying a kind of soft focus, letting what is already there seep in.

usually it starts with a phrase that catches my eye: for example, "like a flower" in "easier heart s," "you forgot you" in "done with misery," or just the word "bees" in "the bees." i then backtrack through the page and find the other pieces that lead to and away from that word, something that connects with me.

other times, it's the arrangement on the original page. the poem for page 277 ("A dream maybe.") was not easy to Find. as a kind of Hail Mary (so to speak), i wrote down all the words that appeared on the left side of the page (nope), then all the words down the middle of the page (not quite), and finally those on the right (yes). the poem lived in that last column.

i think of these poems as collaborations between Julia Peterkin and me. i feel her looking over my shoulder and watching what i'm doing, making suggestions and cuts. i have less control over these poems than i do over my own writing. it's like pulling the loose thread from a sweater: once you start, it doesn't stop. a whole world opens up. it makes for terrible sweaters, but pretty good poems.

8. i want to hold [it in my] hand
there's a handmade quality to *Scarlet Sister Mary*. seemingly every interaction happens while someone is making food, or mending garments, or picking crops. i strove to reflect that tactile feeling in my work. i wanted you to see the marks left behind on each piece: an errant pencil scratch, the stringy end of a piece of gaff tape, a slightly mis-cut corner. in "Night all starlit," i wanted the poem to reflect the craft in a more direct way, using cross stitch to create the blacked out portions of text. i wanted to sweat over each poem and find new ways to present the material over the course of all 30 poems.

9. false starts
the poem for page 73 ("her weakness") is not working. it's got all the elements—smothering fires, a list of animals that could probably be a poem all on its own, even the phrase i try to use every time it appears: "Thank God." but it just doesn't work. i've got five versions, each more deludedly grand than the previous. before i go to bed, out of frustration, i make a smart-alecky set of cuts. i become the boy in the bathroom who scratches out the "on" on the hand dryer so it says "Push Butt."

in the morning, what it looks like instead is taking the apocalyptic and making it personal.

10. Grandma and Grandpa Beaman
only one poem in this collection uses the words out of order. it's also the one poem that represents my active narrative imposition. "eightytwo" is taken from page 82, which also happened to be my Grandmother's age when she passed away. she was also a poet and delighted those around her with her couplets and wordplay. the words in order do not work for what i would like to do. i alphabetize every word on the page[1] and pull phrases from it until it matches her, until the words make me remember her joyful laugh whenever any one of us would come to visit.

Grandma makes another appearance near the end of my Remix month. the photograph in the background of "Heaven" was taken by her, of my Grandfather looking out over Eastern Oregon.[2] if the page was shifted an inch more to the left, you would see him there. once i selected that picture for the background of the poem, the words i sought out spoke more directly to the image and to his passing.

11. I Am the Maker of all sweetened possum
this is a line i found on the page of the very short poem of the same name (and yet was not included in the final poem), and it represents the work in this collection pretty well. each one of these poems is its own slice of sweetened possum. not a dish i would normally seek out, but a unique little unexpected Frankenstein creation completely different from what either a sweet, or a possum would be like.[3]

12. all the rest have 31
when i look back over the entire collection, i don't just see these final versions; i see the poems made from these very same pages that didn't make the cut. some i like just as much, but they didn't fit within the context of the whole. i see the new freedom i found in using Peterkin's words. i see the phrases and ideas i've never contemplated using—even words i didn't know before (hello, terrapins). and i see Peterkin and Mary, lurking behind each work and page, helping me make the sweetened possum, pulling on the loose threads, and ruining our perfectly good sweater.

13. lists
i like them.

14. readers
i also like them. thank you for being them.

[1] a trick i learned from the Fluxus movement.
[2] i believe. please feel free to correct me if i'm wrong, East Oregonians.
[3] okay, it's not a direct one-to-one correlation.

acknowledgments

The source of all text, punctuation and capitalization of the following poems is *Scarlet Sister Mary* by Julia Peterkin.

Special thanks to Jenni B. Baker and the *Found Poetry Review* for including me in the Pulitzer Remix, and to all of my friends and family who selected the pages with which i would work.

Very special thanks to my most trusted reader, editor, and my love, Frances Binder.

biographical note

Julia Peterkin (1880-1961) was born and lived on a plantation in South Carolina, and was a writer of short stories and novels. She was one of the first white authors to write primarily about the African American experience. Her novels include *Green Thursday* (1924), *Black April* (1927), and, of course, *Scarlet Sister Mary* (1928). The latter novel won the Pulitzer Prize in 1929. This award was not without controversy, as one member of the jury resigned in protest. Two of Peterkin's short stories were awarded the O. Henry prize. The Julia Peterkin Award is given in alternating years for poetry or short fiction by Converse College, from which Peterkin graduated and received her Masters (at age 17). Peterkin was also an actress, performing in many plays, including the title role in *Hedda Gabler*.

I Am the Maker of all sweetened possum

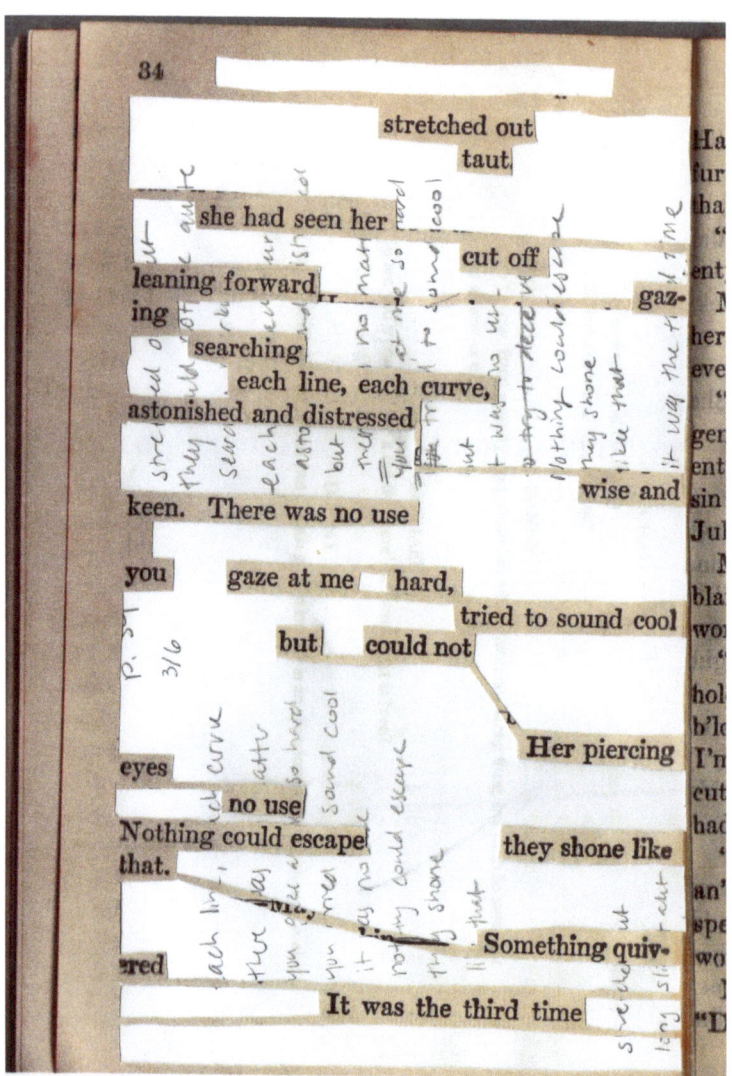

stretched out
taut.
she had seen her
cut off
leaning forward, gaz-
ing
searching
each line, each curve,
astonished and distressed
wise and
keen. There was no use
you gaze at me hard,
tried to sound cool
but could not
Her piercing
eyes
no use
Nothing could escape
that. they shone like
Something quiv-
ered
It was the third time

stretched out taut

stretched out
taut,
she had seen her
cut off
leaning forward gaz-
ing
searching
each line, each curve,
astonished and distressed
wise and
keen. There was no use

you gaze at me hard,
tried to sound cool
but could not

Her piercing
eyes
no use

Nothing could escape
they shone like
that.

Something quiv-
ered

It was the third time

bitterness
was never humble.
caring
was an unforgiving enemy
he loved , he
the world know it.

cut off from
God and
Satan. Every fear
no matter how bold
over and over,
Every time
His
hot
Hell

sought her right here in
this world
She believed
Hell had no doubt
Hell

bound them to each other

straight and strong and able

Hell

                          bitterness
was never humble.
                     caring
           was an unforgiving enemy
                   he loved   , he
let the world know it.

                 cut   off from
                                   God and
Satan. Every   fear
    no matter how bold
        over and over,
            Every time
         His
hot
Hell

             sought her   right here in
this world
She believed
Hell   had no doubt
Hell

             bound them to each other

     straight and strong and able

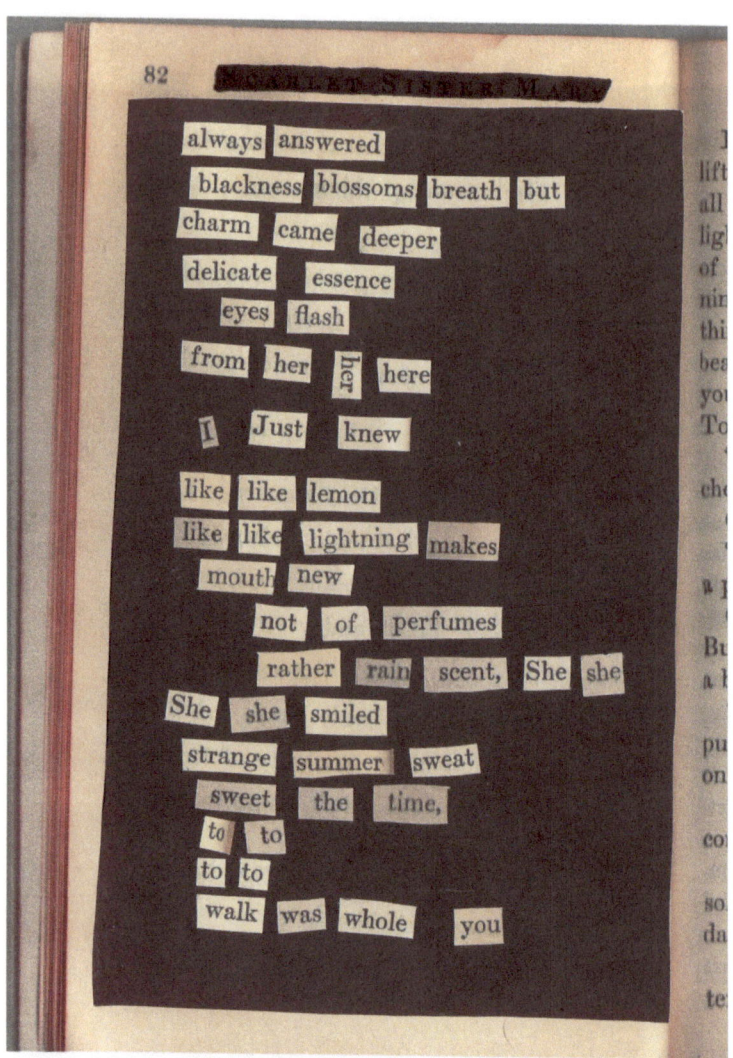

always answered
blackness blossoms breath but
charm came deeper
delicate essence
eyes flash
from her her here
I Just knew
like like lemon
like like lightning makes
mouth new
not of perfumes
rather rain scent, She she
She she smiled
strange summer sweat
sweet the time,
to to
to to
walk was whole you

alphabetized text of page 82

a a a a a a a a a a about although always an' and and and and and and answered any any around as as as at awful
be be beads blackness blossoms breath But but but
came can cat charm chin Cinder Cinder Cinder Cologne cooking coolness crabapple
de de de de deeper delicate do draw dry
ears earrings enty enty essence eyes
field field finger Fire flash food fox 'fraid from from
German get gold gold gold got gwine
had had had heap her Her her her her her here house hot hotness
Hoyt's
I I I I I'd in in in in in In it it's its
jump Just
knew knew
lemon lightnin lightning like like like like likely Look looked looked
lost
made make makes Mary Mary Mary men men mouth much
neck new new not not
of of of of of of of or or older on on one out
perfumes plenty put
quickly
rain rather ready red remarked ring room
scent scent set she She She she she shiny silver skin skinny sly
smelled smiled so some some something spell spite squirrel steadily
stepping straight strange string sudden summer sweat sweet
take teeth that the the the the the the time time to to to to town
walk was was way were whole work would
yonder you'd

warm light over | 192-2
Floods the creaky| door|
opening she| peered out
As soon as she woke to
what into known no everybody else
overs plain enough| everybody else plan en
promised|
the night, lingered in shady
places loath to go| washed + put
shy promises work|
washed and ted put away,
work washed and put away
(trout were biting) trout cared no
the trout cared no
no more | water| coiled | on the
her chapter sunset
alligator
eyes| such creatures
there tad ter-
rapins| sunned themselves in
short int was ne such creatures
Thank God| on be here
So on keep clear made
everybody hug |
short and soon forgotten.
because soon all there with neighbor not
things hot days and work would soon keep
Soon keep clear held face

what was going on.

              warm light over
      the creaky   door
        she   peered out

                            everybody else
     plain enough
      promised
         the night, lingered in shady
places   loath to go
           work
washed and   put away,

the trout   cared
no more   water   coiled   on the
                                 alligator
eyes
                                       ter-
rapins   sunned themselves
                          such creatures

  Thank God,
                                  made
everybody hug
      short and soon forgotten.
    soon
                            soon

sounds stopped for a minute and began.

At last dawn rose, the cocks crowed, the cattle lowed, the birds sang. The flies clustering on the wall-papers woke and hummed and crawled. Mary got up and dressed hurriedly. God had plagued her enough. She would pray until she found peace.

Where could she go and not be seen or heard? The Big House garden held too many ghosts. She hurried down the street, down the hill, toward the thick pine woods. Nobody would find her there. The morning star blazed in the gray east, the night was over. She would spend this day in prayer.

Her misery was not a garment that could be shed. It was mixed in her flesh and blood. Only God could cast it out and heal her.

A deep hush lay at the foot of the pines, but high overhead an early morning breeze moved. She closed her eyes and fell on her knees and bent her head to the earth. But her tongue and lips and voice had got separated and dumb. Despair threatened her. Misery split the shell of her heart clear in two. She could feel it break and bleed. God's mercy was hardened against her and His hand fell heavy on her; thoughts came into her head, but when she tried to hold

high overhead

sounds stopped for a minute.

At last,
the cattle sang
The flies got up and dressed hurriedly.
God had enough.
She held too many ghosts.

hurried down down the hill
the thick pine woods blazed
the night over.

this day
was a garment
mixed in her flesh

God lay at the foot of the pines,
She closed her eyes

Despair   Misery

She could feel it break

God
fell heavy;

thoughts
her head,
she tried
to hold

SCARLET SISTER MARY

The   people   believe they are   the best   people living

lying
with
other
lips   low ways   with

mean blood   and high heads filled with sense.   they have been   fine mechanics   for their

souls.

perfect, intelligent, upstanding human beings

the fine mechanics

The   people
                         believe they are   the
best   people living

lying
with
other
lips   low ways   with

          mean blood
                    and high heads filled with sense.
                                        they have been
                                                fine me-
chanics   for their

          souls.

                                        perfect,
                                intelligent, upstanding
human beings

She had hardly
made *she* made
without herself
that was not so very head
she got weary
she got weary of *deeper things until* when
warm pine straw of tall
thick trees *all* *in* of pleasant things until
a chance
all were forgiven *long steep*
pack of
a long steep
pack of
the *just*
tree *great* h o m e
it stood ache
the burden *right in front*
a great white house,
just it stood in open
w r sunshine right in front
a tall man *e* *d o m*
came out the door and without a word
took the pack
Then *more,*
but burst
no more.
her heart burst

a pack of ache

She had hardly

        made

                            herself

                                  when

  she got weary of
     warm pine straw   of   tall
thick trees   of pleasant things until

       all   were forgiven
             ,

                        a long steep
                        pack of

                            ache
    the burden
        a great white house,
                it stood in   open
      sunshine   right in front
  a tall man
came out   the door and without a word
               took the pack
     Then   ,

       no more.
   her heart   burst

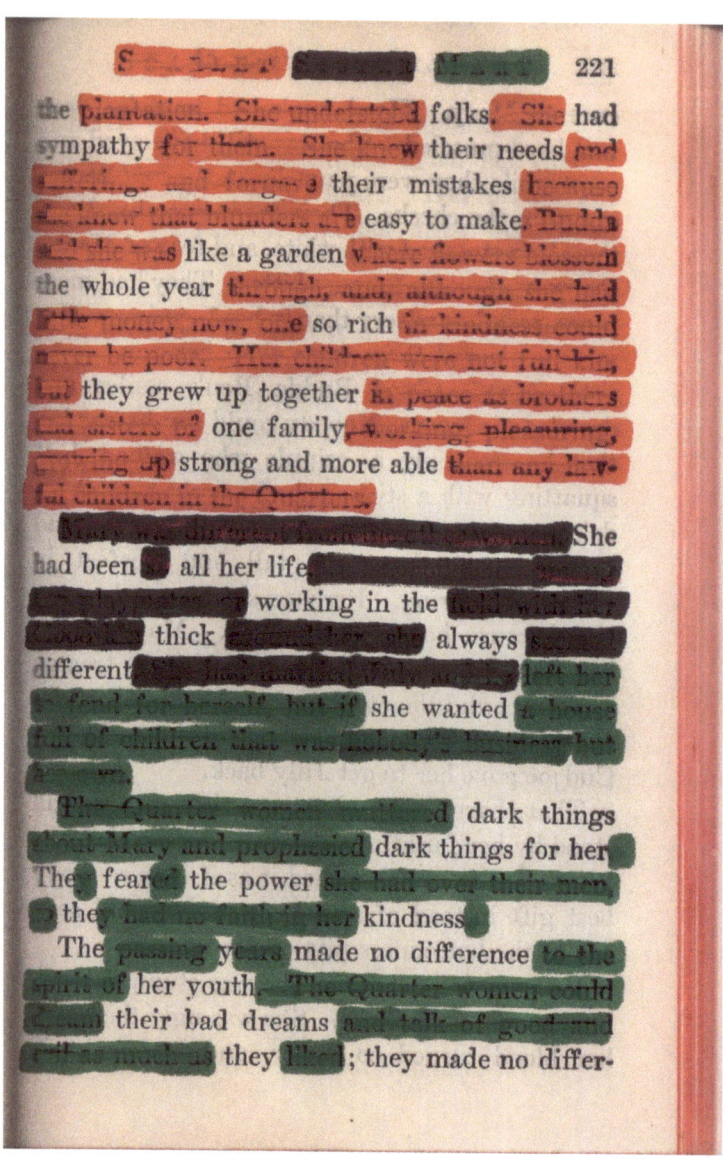

nobody's business

the folks had
sympathy
their needs
their mistakes
easy to make
like a garden
the whole year
so rich

they grew up together
one family
strong and more able

She
had been all her life
working in the
thick always
different
she wanted
dark things
dark things for her
The fear the power
the kindness
The y made no difference
her youth
their bad dreams
they; they made no differ-

her weakness

their lazy
friend Mary
swam about in circles
droning the same tunes over and over
to pester men
until the stench drove them away.
Thank God

alternate version

circles all day long
the same tunes
over and over

the woods were set afire
smothered crickets, frogs, lightning bugs
the sky veiled the fields green
spread and deepened, grew
pinker, brighter, yellow
fierce, growling, thundering
then
passed on
leaving

let
tattered
fires
burn
low

Thank God

the spring
her blood
her weakness

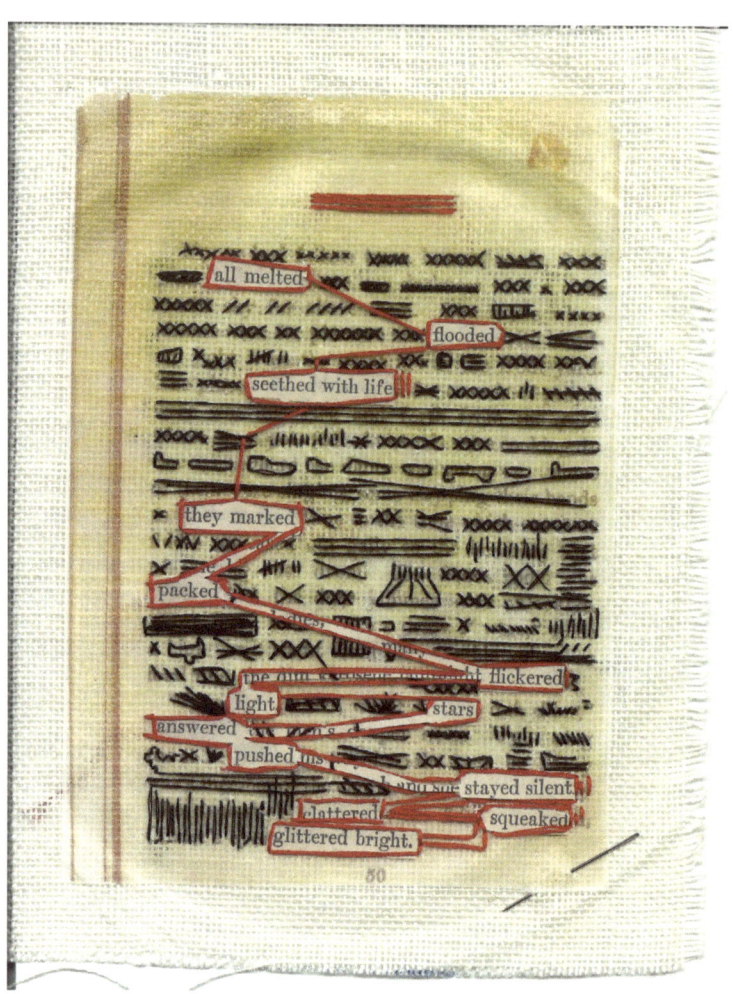

Night all **starlit**

all melted
flooded
seethed with life

they marked
packed
flickered
light

stars
answered
pushed
stayed silent

clattered   squeaked
glittered bright.

to be able to better knuckle to put a hand on that way if it came to the worst plenty of ways grew in the woods; but Sometimes the wrong person had strong sharp teeth one time, one lone time her own sinews like wire; a whip-lash mind over and over gnawing a hole in her heart, a dark place where time got thin, weak ashy and pale.

There were ways

to be able to
better knuckle
to put a
hand on that
way

if it came to the
worst plenty of ways
grew in the woods;

but

Sometimes the wrong person
had strong sharp teeth
one time, one lone time
her own
sinews like wire;
a whip-lash mind
over and over
gnawing a hole
in her heart, a dark place
where time
got thin, weak
ashy and pale.

the world
sighed   soft
and stirred the
         briar patch
         his nostrils
the road
her hands
         Everything
the field rabbit which hurried
   more bad luck

THE road
the river
            the world, the
                    cotton
                        deep ruts
                            side by side
                                where
                            pine-needles
        where every grass-blade
                    was crushed
    by   patient
                    mule hoofs
    the road   the brow   the hill,
                        a
                                cautious
            painstaking curve
                whose roots clutched
                            a
                        dilapidated,
    lonely
            confusion of
    crape-myrtle   gorgeous
                        in every shade

20   CARL

would   drop
   scuffle or   a
             clenched fist
   Yet he loved
                                   both.

            his thick black eyebrows
   his hands doubled up
      like surprise   his eyes

                   big round
          a luck
         in   life
"   I'm   you
" he
                              smiled

                         a trifling
waster   stuck
                                       in
one place   to take root;

                       He would
           would
                                  would
make a fine husband even if he could not

                         see   at night

CARL

would   drop
   a scuffle   or   a
                       clenched fist
Yet he loved
                                      both.

                his thick black eyebrows
      his hands doubled up
           like surprise   his eyes
                            big round
              a luck
              in   life
"   I'm   you ,
" he
                         smiled

                     a trifling
waster   stuck
                                    in
one place   to take root;

                     He would
             would
                         would
make a fine husband even if he could not
                see   at night

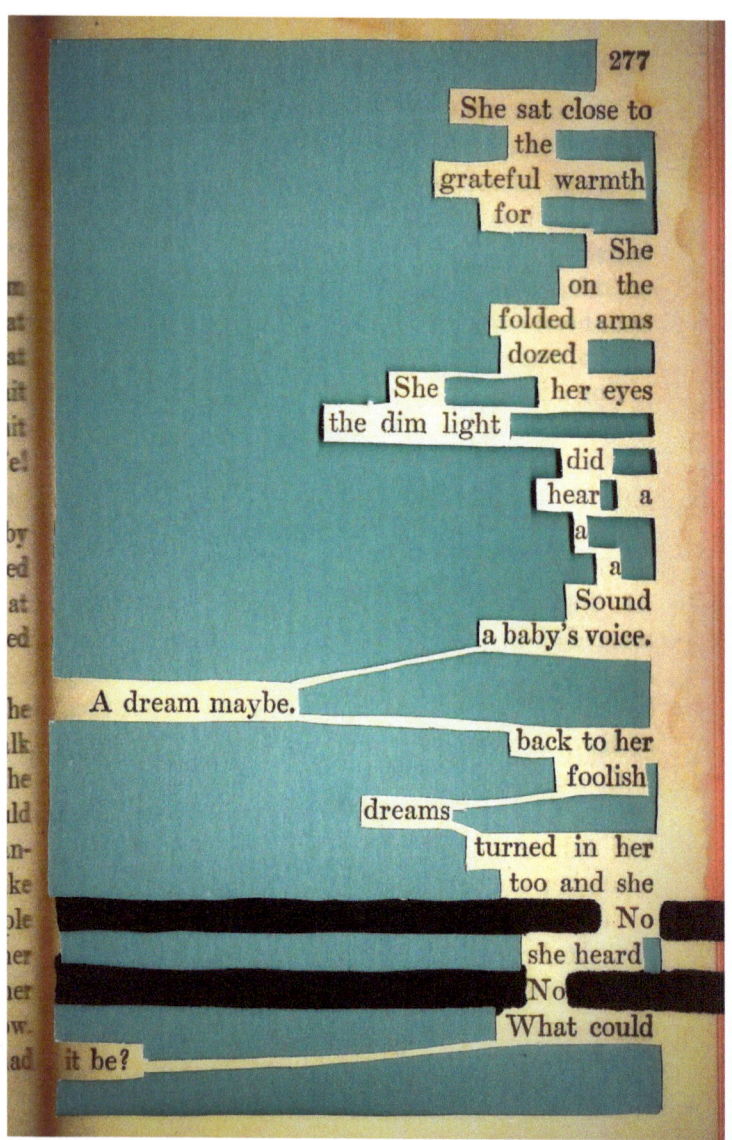

She sat close to
the
grateful warmth
for
She
on the
folded arms
dozed
She her eyes
the dim light
did
hear a
a
a
Sound
a baby's voice.

A dream maybe.
back to her
foolish
dreams
turned in her
too and she
No
she heard
No
What could
it be?

A dream maybe.

She sat close to
the
grateful warmth
for
She
on the
folded arms
dozed
She   her eyes
the dim light
did
hear a
  a
    a
Sound
a baby's voice.

A dream maybe.

back to her
foolish
dreams
turned in her
too and she
         No
she heard
         No
What could
it be?

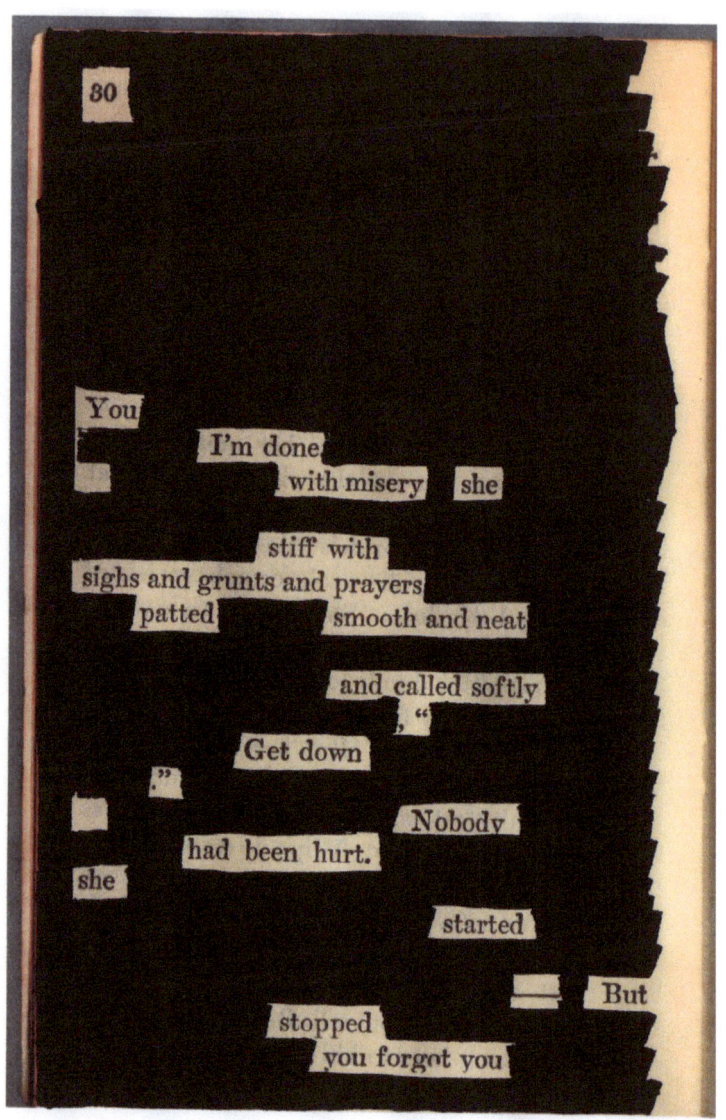

You
 I'm done
  with misery she
    stiff with
sighs and grunts and prayers
   patted   smooth and neat
        and called softly
      "
      Get down
   ."
she had been hurt. Nobody
           started
                But
    stopped
     you forgot you

done with misery

You
      I'm done
          with misery she

        stiff with
sighs and grunts and prayers
    patted   smooth and neat

          and called softly
           ,"
      Get down
."
                Nobody
    had been hurt.
she
        started

              — But
       stopped
         you forgot you

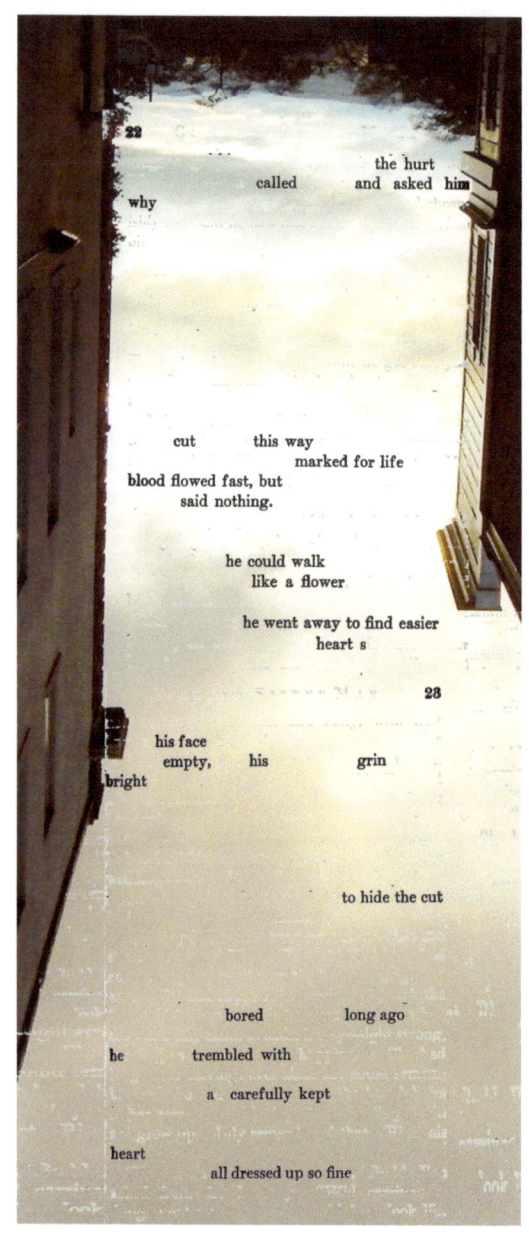

22

the hurt
called and asked him
why

cut this way
marked for life
blood flowed fast, but
said nothing.

he could walk
like a flower

he went away to find easier
heart s

23

his face
empty, his grin
bright

to hide the cut

bored long ago
he trembled with
a carefully kept
heart
all dressed up so fine

easier heart s

the hurt
called and asked him
why

cut this way
marked for life
blood flowed fast, but
said nothing.

he could walk
like a flower

he went away to find easier
heart s

his face
empty, his grin
bright

to hide the cut
bored long ago

he trembled with
a carefully kept
heart

all dressed up so fine

44

plucked

one   boiling   heart
              , honey. It'll do you   good
         fix you someting to
                              never get
                                never
         get loose
         It's   powerful-est   I know
         took a needle
                       took a drop of her   on
a wisp of cotton. "You   strong
         , honey," he said.   catches
     holds.
Then he took a bit of

A bit of toe   from a toe on her left
                                her left
           her heart
       all mixed with some sort of
                scrap of white cloth with a string
long enough
                       His eyes shone and
                his forehead handed
     her   a   crackling.
           "Put 'em on,   Wear em
                     I'll quit makin' love
         rest o' my life.   a man,
                         a mans o monkeys,
honey."

                    her heart began beating

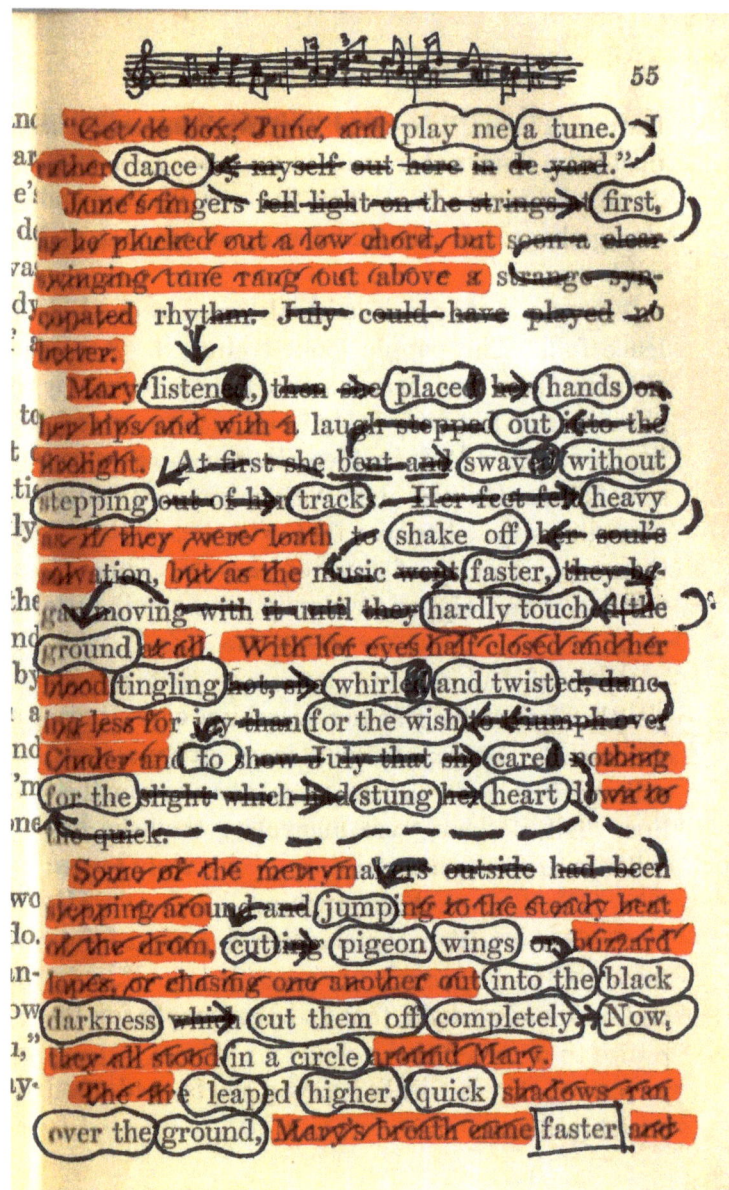

"play me a tune. dance first, swayed without stepping shake off faster, hardly touched ground tingling whirled twisted cared stung heart jumping pigeon wings into the black darkness cut them off completely. leaped higher, quick faster

the dance **steps**

                                               play me a tune.
     dance
                                                    first,

              listen ,   place   hands
                                              out
                                     sway   without
stepping   track   heavy
                             shake off
                                    faster,
                           hardly touch
ground
      tingling   whirl   and twist
                         for the wish
         to   care
for the   stung   heart

                        jump
               cut   pigeon wings
                                into the black
darkness   cut them off completely. Now,
              in a circle
        leap   higher, quick
over the ground,   faster

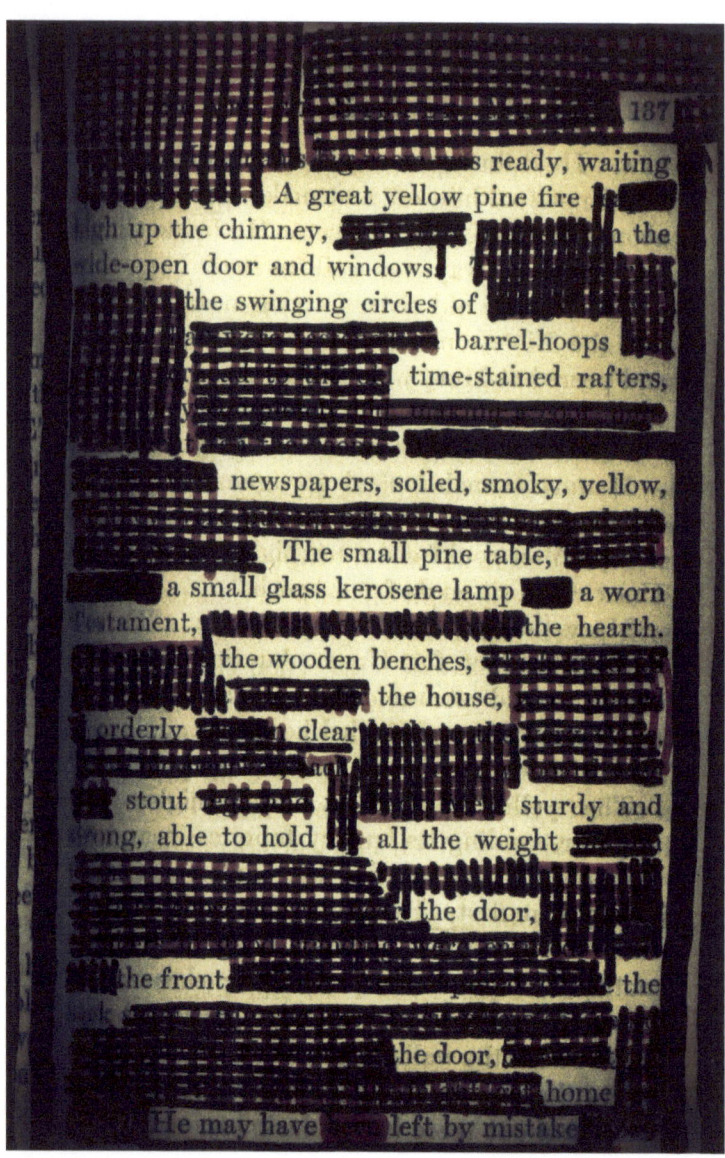

a worn Testament

                              ready, waiting
                A great yellow pine fire
high up the chimney,   the
wide-open door and windows
          the swinging circles of
                              barrel-hoops
                         time-stained rafters,

          newspapers, soiled, smoky, yellow,

                The small pine table,
     a small glass kerosene lamp   a worn
Testament,   the hearth.
               the wooden benches,
                         the house,
     orderly   clear

       stout   sturdy and
strong, able to hold   all the weight

                         the door,

       the front   the
back
                    the door,
                                           home
             He may have   left by mistake

the proud master, now a crumbling shell with broken chimney rotting roof a rattling window blind the tall cedars and magnolias to tumble down make living an easy thing footprint years determined to break to quake tumble down trees and houses, bones cruelty burn with impartial cruelty, but every scar is fill empty quickly built to fill empty spaces Life enfolds the most insignificant creature, a silent, strange miracle s o death becomes another beginning.

another beginning

the proud
master, now a crumbling shell with
broken chimney   rotting roof
a   rattling   window
blind
the tall
cedars and magnolias
make living an easy thing
footprint S
years   determined to break
to quake tumble down
trees and houses,
bones
burn with impar-
tial cruelty, but
every scar is
quickly built
to fill empty
spaces

Life enfolds
the
most insignificant creature, a   si-
lent ,
strange miracle   s o
death becomes   another be-
ginning.

I Am the Maker of all sweetened possum

Men are like children when things go wrong.

SCARLET SISTER MARY 111

break her back ▓▓▓▓ her ▓▓▓▓ good husband ▓▓▓ had never come back ▓▓▓

▓▓▓ a hen's anxious clucking chicken ▓▓▓▓ voice asked ▓▓, "Honey — is you sleepin?"

▓▓▓ she felt ▓▓▓▓ every body crying and wishing ▓▓▓

"No ▓▓ sleep. ▓▓▓ headache. ▓▓▓ it's so awful ▓▓▓ hardly catch enough air."

"▓▓▓▓▓▓ come look ▓▓▓ blue hen stole a ▓▓▓ chimney and hatched ▓▓▓ all blue ▓▓ as can be. ▓ blue hen's ▓▓ lucky, so ▓▓▓ you ▓ see ▓

▓ feed em; ▓ Let em sleep ▓▓▓
▓▓▓ put them down in a dark ▓▓ room and carefully cover ▓ them ▓; then she sat down, took her pipe out

the hotness for life

break her back her
good husband had
never come back

a hen's anxious clucking
chicken voice
asked, "Honey – is you sleepin?"

she felt
everybody
crying and wishing

"No sleep. headache.
it's so awful
hardly catch
enough air."

"
come look
blue hen stole a chimney
and hatched all blue
as can be. blue hen's
lucky, so you see
feed em, Let em sleep
"

put them down in a dark
room and carefully cover them
; then she sat down, took her pipe out

Scarlet Sister Mary

Mary must have   not   brought
                        everybody
                his son   Mary
had never heard

          The baby
They   call him   a nice name,
a pleasant-sounding name.
                    a   baby never came
into the world   Mary's heart
       was full of
nothing

SCARLET SISTER MARY

Mary must have not brought
everybody his son

Mary had never heard
The baby

They call him a nice name,
a pleasant-sounding name.

a baby never came
into the world

Mary's heart
was full
of nothing

alternate version

                                      he brought
                                      everybody
                                        a dress
           Unexpected

       it meant
                that very thing
                        a nice

a pleasant-sounding
     world
          full of
   nothing

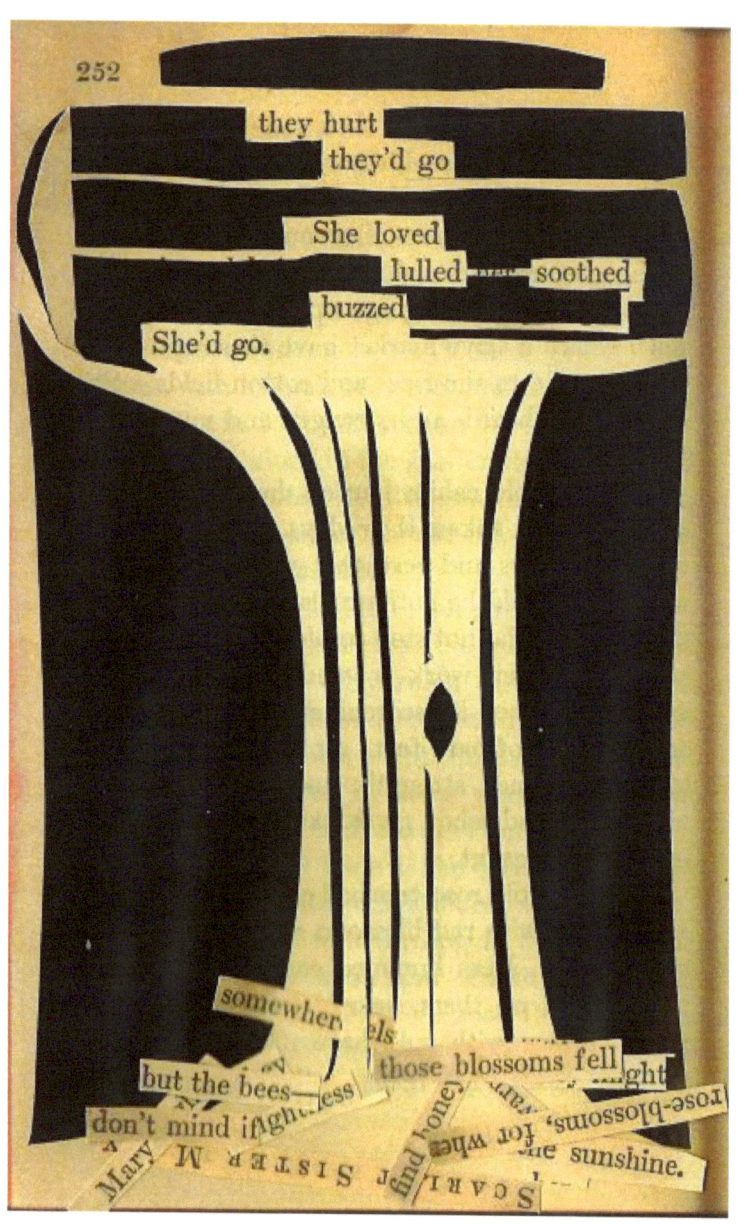

they hurt
they'd go

She loved
lulled soothed
buzzed
She'd go.

somewhere
but the bees those blossoms fell
don't mind if sunshine.

the bees

they hurt
they'd go

She loved
lulled soothed
buzzed

She'd go.

270 SCARLET SISTER MARY

h   e   grinning   like a boar
hog, rose   out of
                    the awful

    H   e   smaller than
all of them
                in front of the fire waving
                making horrible faces
                        afraid to look at
                        her child
                        her eyes
        h   i   s   dropped
    , one at a time,
                    up   and
            down
until they turned to little black creatures
                        he   hopped and
hopped around   /   the fire until
            he wanted to cry.
he had heard   , but
    had never understood how awful it was
now   all those
terrible things
Some of them   some of them
                were
        comfort

comfort

<pre>
h   e   grinning   like a boar
hog, rose   out of
                         the awful
                              .
      H   e   smaller than
all of them
                         in front of the fire waving
                            making horrible faces
                                 afraid to look at
                                 her child
                                 her eyes
           h   i   s   dropped
       , one at a time,
                         up   and
                      down
until they turned to little black creatures
                                  he   hopped and
hopped around   the fire until
                        he wanted to cry.
   he had heard   , but
       had never understood how awful it was
now
                                      all those
terrible things
Some of them   some of them
                         were
                         comfort
</pre>

And yet

Heaven's a long ways home. Heaven's a might certain place

when you get to Heaven I'm waitin for you, set right by you "I hope so. I hope The cool air outside was all the more pleasant with its black coal smoke, he breathed it deep before he started walking leading New fragrant weeds reaching up to all the yellow breeze of summer floated he swept it away, then climbed up

Heaven

And yet

Heaven's
a long ways home.

Heaven's a
might certain
place

when you get to Heaven I'm
waitin for you, set right by you

"I hope so. I hope."

The cool air outside was
all the more pleasant
with its black coal
smoke   he breathed it deep
before he started walking
leading
New fragrant weeds
reaching up to all the
yellow   breeze   of   summer
   floated
      he
         swept it away, then climbed up

about the author

photo by Frances Binder

james w. moore is a writer of poetry, plays, and short stories. his poetry has appeared in the *Found Poetry Review*, the Silver Birch Press *Noir Erasure Poetry Anthology*, the *Houston Chronicle* and on Vermont Edition. five of his full-length plays have received world premieres, including original works such as *cart* (which American Theatre magazine called "a wonderfully surreal comedy"), and adaptations of *Robin Hood* and *Rapunzel* for the Northwest Children's Theater. he was twice awarded residencies at Caldera Arts, and his one act play *Ubu's Last Krapp* was featured as part of the End of the Pavement series. his work has been performed in Chicago (SOLO Festival), Seattle (On the Boards), Portland (Oregon—PICA's TBA Festival and JAW), and in Burlington, Vermont. he currently lives and creates in Winooski, Vermont.

www.ingramcontent.com/pod-product-compliance
Lightning Source LLC
Chambersburg PA
CBHW041528090426
42736CB00036B/228